Rhythm Workbook
Level Two
For Piano, Electronic Keyboard or Organ
by Wesley Schaum

FOREWORD

This book is planned as a supplement to a **level two** method book. It can be used by students of *all ages*, children, teenagers and adults. The purpose is to help develop an understanding and feeling for fundamental rhythms.

Practical, step-by-step progression correlates note and rest recognition with counting, rhythmic drills, various time signatures and measure construction. Although this book is primarily intended to reinforce the teaching of rhythms, extra benefits can be derived by having the student use these lessons as note reading exercises.

This edition has completely new music engraving designed to improve the visual image of counting and rhythms based on suggestions submitted by Alfred Cahn of Milwaukee, Wisconsin.

Other Schaum Workbooks:

Level Two
Theory Workbook, Level 2
Easy Keyboard Harmony, Book 1
Scale Speller

Level Three
Theory Workbook, Level 3
Rhythm Workbook, Level 3
Argeggio Speller
Easy Keyboard Harmony, Book 2

Level Four
Theory Workbook, Level 4
Interval Speller
Easy Keyboard Harmony, Book 3
Rhythm Workbook, Level 4

Exclusively Distributed By

HAL•LEONARD® CORPORATION

7777 W. BLUEMOUND RD. P.O. BOX 13819 MILWAUKEE, WI 53213

02-23

INDEX – Level Two

INDEX – Level Three

Lesson 1.   Time Signature Review

Name _____   Date _____   Score _____

2 ← 2 counts
4   per measure

3 ← 3 counts
4   per measure

4 ← 4 counts
4   per measure

A QUARTER note gets one count.

DIRECTIONS: The measures below have missing *time signatures*. Write in the counting for each measure. Then write in the correct time signature at the beginning of each measure.

(sample)   1   2   3   +

– – – – – – – – – –   – – – – – – – – – –   – – – – – – – – – –

– – – – – – – – – –   – – – – – – – – – –   – – – – – – – – – –

– – – – – – – – – –   – – – – – – – – – –   – – – – – – – – – –

– – – – – – – – – –   – – – – – – – – – –   – – – – – – – – – –

– – – – – – – – – –   – – – – – – – – – –   – – – – – – – – – –

RHYTHM DRILL: After writing in the counting above, *count aloud* (according to the time signature) and *clap hands* – one clap for each note. Count aloud for the *rests*, but do not clap.

Lesson 2.   Review of Note and Rest Counting

Name _____   Date _____   Score _____

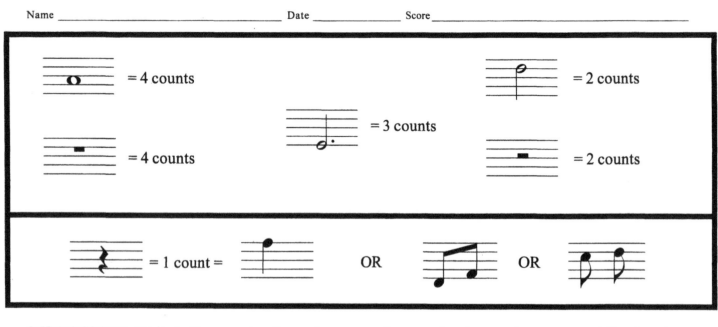

DIRECTIONS: Write in the counting for each measure. Be sure that the numbers are carefully placed *directly below* the note or rest to which they apply.

RHYTHM DRILL: When finished, *count aloud* and *clap hands* (as in Lesson 1).

Lesson 3.   Upbeat (or "Pickup") Notes

Name _____   Date _____   Score _____

> An UPBEAT (or "Pickup") occurs when the first note of a piece is NOT the first *count* of a measure.*
>
> An "Upbeat" can occur with *any* time signature.

DIRECTIONS: Draw a circle around the "UPBEAT" notes in each line of music below. Then, write in the counting on the dotted lines for every measure (see sample). Watch for *different* time signatures.

(sample)   4

(Circle the *upbeat* notes, then write in the counting.)

(Reminder: Watch for *different* time signatures.)

*The counts missing at the beginning of a piece are often (but not always) made up in the final measure of the piece. This depends upon the individual composer or arranger.

Lesson 4.   Upbeat Notes with Missing Measure Bars

Name _____   Date _____   Score _____

DIRECTIONS: Draw a circle around the "UPBEAT" notes in each line of music below. Next, write in the counting on the dotted lines. Then, draw in bar lines where necessary so that each measure will have the correct number of counts.

Symbol for Common Time (same as 4/4 time)

(Circle the *upbeat* notes, write in the counting, then draw in measure bar lines.)

(Reminder: Write in the counting numbers *directly below* the note or rest to which they apply.)

RHYTHM DRILL: When finished, *count aloud* and *clap hands* – one clap for each note. Count aloud for the *rests*, but do not clap.

Lesson 5.   Counting Notes on Leger Lines

Name _____ Date _____ Score _____

> Notes written on LEGER LINES or in LEGER SPACES (above or below either staff) are counted the SAME as notes written in the staff.

DIRECTIONS: Write in the counting on the dotted lines for every measure.

(Write in the counting.)

(Reminder: Watch for *different* time signatures.)

Lesson 6.   Dotted Quarter and Single Eighth Notes

Name _____ Date _____ Score _____

A DOTTED QUARTER note is equal to one QUARTER note tied to one EIGHTH note.

A DOTTED QUARTER note is *counted the same* as one QUARTER note tied to one EIGHTH note.

DIRECTIONS: Write in the counting on the dotted lines for every measure.

_ _

(Write in the counting.)

TEACHER'S NOTE: When writing in the counting, "and" may be abbreviated with an ampersand (&) instead of a plus sign (+) if desired.

Lesson 7. Eighth Rest Counting

Name _____ Date _____ Score _____

This is an EIGHTH REST.
It is counted the same as an Eighth Note.

This is an Eighth Rest in the Staff.

DIRECTIONS: On the staffs below, some of the measure bar lines are missing. Write in the counting on the dotted lines. Then draw in bar lines where necessary so that each mesure will have the correct number of counts.

(sample)   2   1   2   +

(Write in the counting, then draw in measure bar lines.)

RHYTHM DRILL: When finished, *count aloud* and *clap hands* (as in Lesson 4).

Lesson 8. 6/8 Time Signature

Name _____ Date _____ Score _____

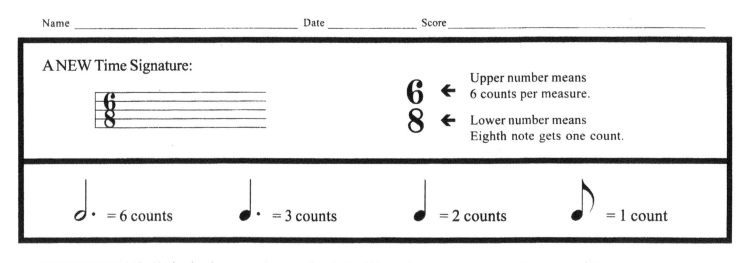

DIRECTIONS: Write in the counting on the dotted lines for every measure (see sample).

(sample)   1   2   3   4   5   6

(Write in the counting - *six counts* per measure.)

Lesson 9.   6/8 Counting

Name _____ Date _____ Score _____

DIRECTIONS: On the staffs below, some of the measure bar lines are missing. Write in the counting on the dotted lines. Then draw in the bar lines so that each measure will have six counts.

(Write in the counting, then draw in measure bar lines.)

(Reminder: Write in the counting numbers *directly below* the note or rest to which they apply.)

RHYTHM DRILL: When finished, *count aloud* and *clap hands* (as in Lesson 4). In the bottom line of music, do the treble clef counting alone, then do the bass clef counting alone.

Lesson 10.   Rest Values in 6/8 Time

Name _____ Date _____ Score _____

A REST may be DOTTED, the same as a note.

Other RESTS in 6/8 Time:

DIRECTIONS: Write in the counting on the dotted lines for every measure.

(Write in the counting - *six counts* per measure.)

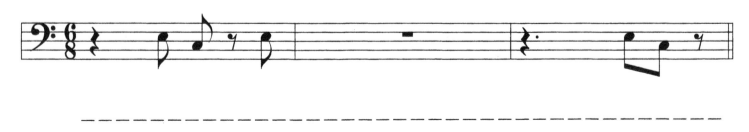

Lesson 11.   6/8 Counting with Rests

Name _____ Date _____ Score_____

DIRECTIONS: On the staffs below, some of the measure bar lines are missing. Write in the counting on the dotted lines. Then draw in the bar lines so that each measure will have six counts.

(Write in the counting, then draw in measure bar lines.)

(Note: In 6/8 time, the WHOLE rest gets SIX counts.)

RHYTHM DRILL: When finished, *count aloud* and *clap hands* (as in Lesson 4). In the two bottom lines of music, do the treble clef counting alone, then do the bass clef counting alone.

Lesson 12.   Staccato and Extension Dots

Name _____ Date _____ Score _____

Notice differences between musical DOTS:

STACCATO dot    EXTENSION dot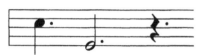

1. Used ONLY with NOTES

2. Always directly ABOVE or
   BELOW the note head

3. Does NOT change the counting

4. Note is played in a DETACHED,
   SEPARATED manner

1. Used with RESTS and NOTES

2. Always on the RIGHT SIDE
   of the note or rest

3. LENGTHENS the time value
   of the note or rest by ONE HALF

4. Note is played in the normal manner

DIRECTIONS: Draw a *red* circle around all STACCATO dots. Draw a *green* circle around all EXTENSION dots.

TEACHER'S NOTE: Crayon, ball-point pen or colored pencil may be used by the student. If the specified color is not available, the teacher may designate a substitute.

Lesson 13.   Counting with Staccato and Extension Dots

Name _____ Date _____ Score _____

DIRECTIONS: Write in the counting for each measure. Watch for staccato dots and extension dots. Also watch for *different* time signatures.

(sample)   1   2 + 3 + 4

(Reminder: Watch for *different* time signatures.)

RHYTHM DRILL: When finished, *count aloud* and *clap hands* (as in Lesson 4). In the two bottom lines of music, do the treble clef counting alone, then do the bass clef counting alone.

Lesson 14.   Identifying Ties and Slurs

Name _____ Date _____ Score _____

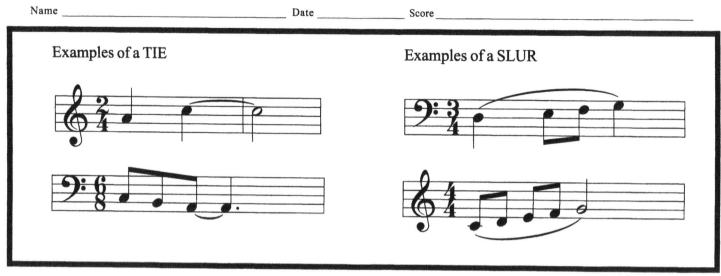

Examples of a TIE   Examples of a SLUR

DIRECTIONS: On the dotted lines *between the staffs*, write the word TIE or SLUR depending upon where the arrow is pointing (see sample).

(sample)   **TIE**

(Write in the word TIE or SLUR.)

Lesson 15.   Counting with Ties and Slurs

Name _____   Date _____   Score _____

DIRECTIONS: On the staffs below, some of the measure bar lines are missing. Write in the counting on the dotted lines below each measure. Then draw in the bar lines where necessary so that each measure will have the correct number of counts.

(Write in the counting, then draw in measure bar lines.)

(Reminder: Write in the counting numbers *directly below* the note or rest to which they apply.)

RHYTHM DRILL: When finished, *count aloud* and *clap hands* (as in Lesson 4). In the two bottom lines of music, do the treble clef counting alone, then do the bass clef counting alone.

TEACHER'S NOTE: When writing in the counting, "and" may be abbreviated with an ampersand (&) instead of a plus sign (+) if desired.

Lesson 16.   3/8 Time Signature

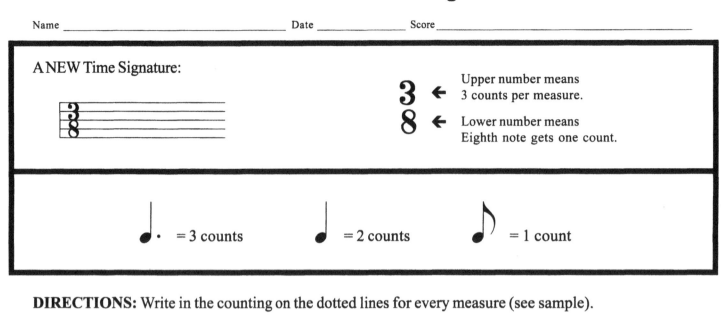

A NEW Time Signature:

3 ← Upper number means 3 counts per measure.

8 ← Lower number means Eighth note gets one count.

♩. = 3 counts   ♩ = 2 counts   ♪ = 1 count

DIRECTIONS: Write in the counting on the dotted lines for every measure (see sample).

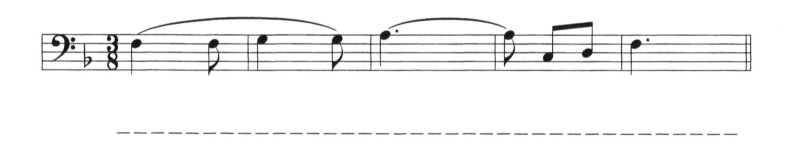

(sample)   1   2   3

(Write in the counting - *three counts* per measure.)

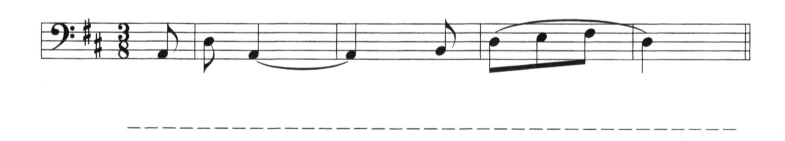

Lesson 17.   3/8 Counting with Rests

Name _____ Date _____ Score_____

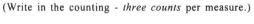
DIRECTIONS: Write in the counting on the dotted lines for every measure (see sample).

(sample)   1   2   3
– –

(Write in the counting - *three counts* per measure.)

– –

(Reminder: Write in the counting numbers *directly below* the note or rest to which they apply.)

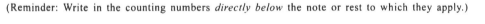

– –

– –

RHYTHM DRILL: When finished, *count aloud* and *clap hands* (as in Lesson 4).

Lesson 18.   Adding Rests in 3/8 and 6/8 Time

Name _____ Date _____ Score _____

DIRECTIONS: In the measures below, *rests* have been left out. Draw in rests where necessary to make the correct number of counts in each treble and bass clef measure. Then write in the counting on the dotted lines.

(Draw in the *rests* as needed, then write in the counting.)

(Reminder: Watch for *different* time signatures.)

Lesson 19.   Difference between 3/4 and 3/8 Time

Name _____ Date _____ Score _____

Notice the difference between 3/4 and 3/8 Time.
Both indicate 3 counts per measure.

Lower number means
Quarter Note gets one count.

Lower number means
Eighth Note gets one count.

DIRECTIONS: On the staffs below, the measure bar lines are missing. Write in the counting on the dotted lines. Then draw in the bar lines where necessary so that each measure will have three counts. Watch for *different* time signatures.

(Write in the counting, then draw in measure bar lines.)

(Reminder: Write in the counting numbers *directly below* the note or rest to which they apply.)

RHYTHM DRILL: When finished, *count aloud* and *clap hands* (as in Lesson 4).

Lesson 20.   Natural Accents

Name _____ Date _____ Score _____

When playing music, you may be aware of a small pulse on the first count of every measure. This is called a **natural accent**. It is more an *internal feeling* than an actual accent. It helps you to maintain a steady beat and organize the rhythm in your mind. Natural accents occur:

In 2/4 Time .... on 1st count   In 4/4 Time .... on 1st and 3rd counts

In 3/4 Time .... on 1st count   In 6/8 Time .... on 1st and 4th counts

Natural accents are sometimes called *strong beats*. Other counts in a measure are normal beats (sometimes called *weak beats*).

DIRECTIONS: Write in the counting on the dotted lines for every measure. Then draw a circle around the numbers that are natural accents (see samples).

(sample)   ①   2   ③   4   +

(Write in the counting, then circle the natural accent.)

(sample)   ①   2   3

Lesson 21.   Syncopated Patterns

Name _____   Date _____   Score _____

Syncopation is a rhythm that moves the accent away from the natural accent. A syncopation usually occurs between the numbered beats. Syncopated patterns are indicated with a red bracket. The syncopated beat is circled with red.

Notice that the counting and rhythm in the 1st and 2nd measures is the same, although the note values are different. The counting and rhythm in the 4th and 5th measures is also the same.

These syncopated patterns may occur on any count in measures of 2/4, 3/4 and 4/4 time. Sometimes the tie may cross a bar line.

DIRECTIONS: Write in the counting on the dotted lines for every measure. Syncopated patterns are indicated with a red bracket. Draw a circle around each count where there is a syncopated beat. If necessary, refer to the examples above.

(sample)   1 (+) 2 + 3   4

(Write in the counting, then circle the syncopated beat.)

Lesson 22. Additional Examples of Syncopation

Name _____ Date _____ Score _____

DIRECTIONS: On the staffs below, the bar lines are missing. The measures have examples of SYNCO-PATION. Write in the counting on the dotted lines. Then draw in bar lines where necessary so that each measure will have the correct number of counts.

(Write in the counting, then draw in measure bar lines.)

(Reminder: Watch for *different* time signatures.)

RHYTHM DRILL: When finished, *count aloud* and *clap hands* (as in Lesson 4). In the two bottom lines of music, do the treble clef counting alone, then do the bass clef counting alone.

Lesson 23. Sixteenth Note Identification

Name _____ Date _____ Score _____

These are SIXTEENTH notes.

They are similar to Eighth Notes except their stems are joined by TWO heavy lines (double beams).

Double Beams
↓

↑
Notice Double Beams

DIRECTIONS: Draw a circle around each group of SIXTEENTH notes.

(sample)

(Circle each group of 16th notes.)

Lesson 24. Sixteenth Note Counting: 3/8 and 6/8 Time

Name _____ Date _____ Score _____

TWO Sixteenth Notes together are counted the same as ONE Eighth Note.

```
1   +   2        3   +   1   +   2   +   3
```

DIRECTIONS: Write in the counting on the dotted lines for every measure (see sample).

(sample)   1   +   2   +   3   4   5   6   +
- -

(Write in the counting - watch for *different* time signatures.)

Lesson 25.   16th and 8th Notes Beamed Together

Name _____   Date _____   Score _____

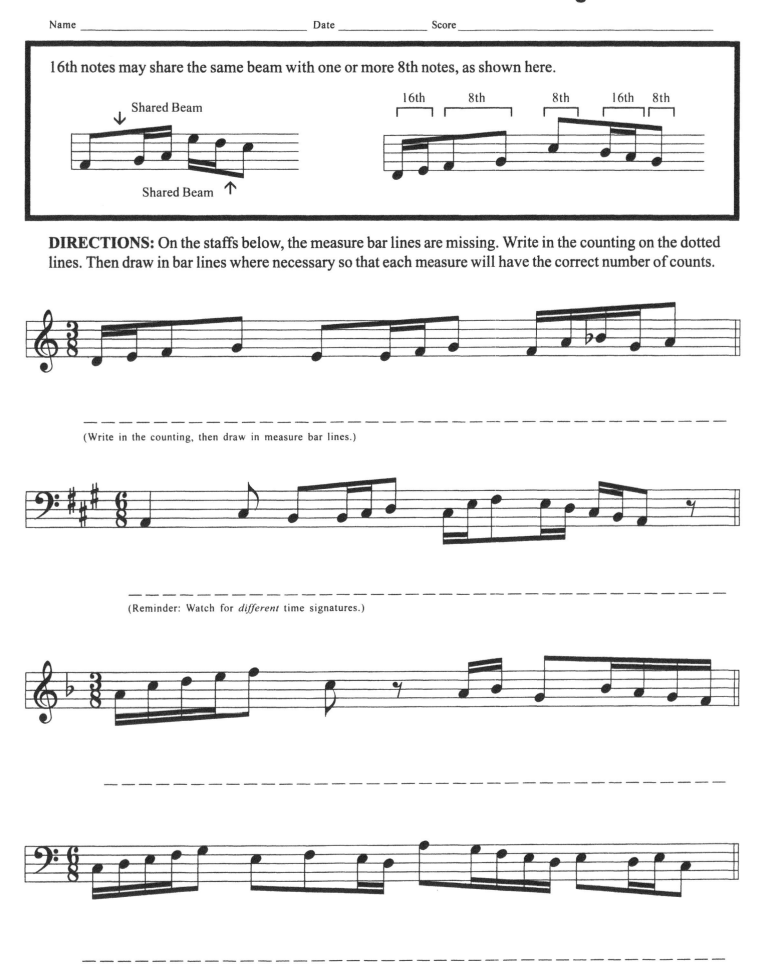

16th notes may share the same beam with one or more 8th notes, as shown here.

DIRECTIONS: On the staffs below, the measure bar lines are missing. Write in the counting on the dotted lines. Then draw in bar lines where necessary so that each measure will have the correct number of counts.

(Write in the counting, then draw in measure bar lines.)

(Reminder: Watch for *different* time signatures.)

RHYTHM DRILL: After completing the written work, *count aloud* and *clap hands* for each line of music (as in Lesson 4).

Lesson 26. 16th Note Counting – Quarter Note Unit

Name _____ Date _____ Score _____

---

*In 2/4 time, 16th notes are counted as shown here. Counting of 16th notes is similar in 3/4 and 4/4 time.

1 e + a 2 e + a 1 e + 2 e + 1 + a 2 + a

DIRECTIONS: Write in the counting on the dotted lines for every measure.

(Write in the counting.)

(Reminder: Watch for *different* time signatures.)

*TEACHER'S NOTE: The counting shown above is pronounced "one - ee - and - ah" etc. If desired, you may substitute different syllables. However, it is recommended that the plus sign *always* be pronounced "*and.*"

Lesson 27.   16th Note Counting – Inserting Bar Lines

Name _____ Date _____ Score _____

DIRECTIONS: On the staffs below, some of the measure bar lines are missing. Write in the counting on the dotted lines. Then draw in bar lines where necessary so that each measure will have the correct number of counts.

(Write in the counting, then draw in bar lines.)

(Reminder: Watch for *different* time signatures.)

RHYTHM DRILL: When finished, *count aloud* and *clap hands* (as in Lesson 4). In the bottom two lines of music, do the treble clef counting alone, then do the bass clef counting alone.

Lesson 28. 16th Note Counting – with 8th and Quarter Note Units

Name _____ Date _____ Score_____

DIRECTIONS: Write in the counting on the dotted lines for every measure. *Watch carefully!* In some time signatures the QUARTER note gets one count. In others, the EIGHTH note gets one count.

- -

(Write in the counting - watch for different time signatures.)

- -

(Reminder: In some time signatures the QUARTER note gets one count. In others, the EIGHTH note gets one count.)

RHYTHM DRILL: When finished, *count aloud* and *clap hands* (as in Lesson 4). In the bottom two lines of music, do the treble clef counting alone, then do the bass clef counting alone.

Lesson 29.   Time Signature Identification

Name _____ Date _____ Score _____

The UPPER number of a Time Signature indicates *how many counts* there are in each measure.

$\frac{2}{4}$ $\frac{3}{4}$ $\frac{4}{4}$ **C** $\frac{3}{8}$ $\frac{6}{8}$

The LOWER number indicates *what kind of note* gets one count.

If LOWER number is 4 – a *quarter* notes gets one count.
If LOWER number is 8 – an *eighth* note gets one count.

DIRECTIONS: The measures below have missing *time signatures*. Write in the counting for each measure. Then write in the correct time signature at the beginning of each measure.

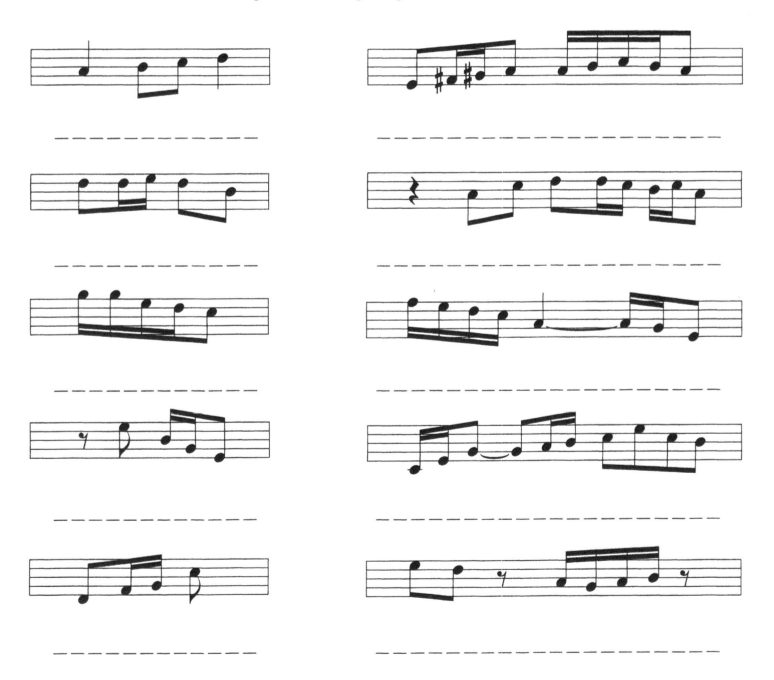

TEACHER'S NOTE: It is possible that the student might not differentiate between measures of 3/4 and 6/8 time. It may be necessary to point out how the beaming of note groups usually differs with these time signatures. In the above lesson, the student should find TWO measures of 3/4 and TWO measures of 6/8 time.

Lesson 30. Rhythm Quiz

Name _____ Date _____ Score _____

DIRECTIONS: Match each musical sign with its description by placing the corresponding alphabetical letter on the line beside the description.

A	(2/4 time)	I	(two eighth notes beamed)
B	(half rest)	J	(common time C)
C	(staccato dotted note)	K	(dotted quarter rest)
D	(slurred notes)	L	(6/8 time)
E	(eighth rest)	M	(dotted note)
F	(3/8 time)	N	(notes with sixteenth beams)
G	(beamed notes)	O	(tied notes)
H	(whole rest)	P	(sixteenth note group)

__E__ Eighth Rest
(sample)

_____ Six Counts per Measure

_____ Notes Connected by a TIE

_____ Eighth Notes

_____ Half Rest

_____ Three Counts per Measure

_____ Whole Rest

_____ Staccato Dot

_____ A Measure of 3/8 Time

_____ Notes Connected by a SLUR

_____ Sixteenth Notes

_____ Four Counts per Measure

_____ Dotted Quarter Rest

_____ Two Counts per Measure

_____ Extension Dot

_____ A Measure of 6/8 Time

TEACHER'S NOTE: Some examples may have more than one correct answer, therefore, some letters may be used more than once.

You are now ready to progress to Schaum's RHYTHM WORKBOOK, Level 3.